TWISTS

Gathered Ephemera

by darrell parry

**Published by Parisian Phoenix Publishing,
Easton, Pennsylvania USA**

Cover Art by Maryann Riker

Interior art created by the author

PARISIAN PHOENIX
PUBLISHING

C O N N E C T with the publisher:
 ParisianPhoenix
 parisbirdbooks
www.ParisianPhoenix.com

Foreword

When Darrell shared that he was working on a book — in that casual way that he shares significant things — I thought about the fact that he hadn't done this before. I took pause.

Darrell is the type of person who yields his time, and lets others have space.

Most poets decide at some point that it is time to share poems in print, drawing from their body of work to create a collection. There is something about that "first book." While it is true that we have heard some of these before, there is something really significant about committing them to a page that can be shared. I read these poems quietly, alone, and experienced them differently. His work deserves this archive. His poetry deserves space.

Every person in Darrell's life will recognize different things in his poetry, and those who know him well will likely find connections to what he honors and will be reminded that these observations of the everyday are what he mines. This is what I relate to most about him, the active "seeing" of the ordinary. His poems remind me of the way we talk: objects like characters. When he mentions the plant, I know that he means the one that thrives in spite of him. There is the kitchen towel of a mother's love. There is the white cup. When he writes about eggs, he expresses their passive vexing. When he vacuums in the dark, I can see him doing this and I know that I would be pacing around by the switch. And he knows that I would be, but he would find humor in it because he knows now that it says more about others than it says about him. You will know which type you are, and that is what he does in his poems. Even when he is sharing his thoughts, he is acknowledging an anonymous reader out there and giving space. And in it, you will be asked to own your shit. He won't ask it, you will.

Even when the tone is sad, he is thinking about you, adding humor. He is that person who worries about making things awkward, so he reassures. He laughs first.

He is the guy you root for, the guy that you can't stay angry at, because you are angry on his behalf about something that he is not bothered by at all. So often, he writes about doing

i

things wrong, and yet we come away with reminders about arrogant intolerance. He manages to flip "wrongness" back around without us realizing it. Until we've realized it.

These poems have vulnerability, candor, and a blend of levity and lightness with serious themes that have come to be his style. He has gone to battle with self doubt, and is sharing what he knows: that weird not only finds weird, but values it. If I could speak for his friends in the poetry community, I know that we wouldn't have him any other way.

— E. Lynn Alexander, cofounder of Collapse Press
and cohost of the Lehigh Valley Poetry Salon

Publisher's Note

I met Darrell Parry in the student union building at Moravian College — where he started his academic career as an art major, though not by choice. By sophomore year, we had mutual friends and English majors and I learned that Darrell had been writing and constructing his own poetry chapbooks since high school.

We're both published poets now, though poetry is not my natural genre. There's something magical about the artistic economization of words that I appreciate, but I'm also extremely critical so I tend to see too many poets not trying hard enough to add something beautiful and unique to the annals of poetry.

Darrell is not a naturally observant person — not in the sense of "where did I leave my car keys" or "what store has ground beef at the lowest price?" but he's attuned to the majestic and personal details of life for himself and others, even when he doesn't know how to change them.

I know this, because Darrell and I were married for 20 years, have a lovely and wicked teenager daughter, and despite the fact that we have been separated for more than two years, there's an unspoken agreement between us that we will always support each other.

So when my cofounder and I launched Parisian Phoenix, it seemed only natural that Darrell should write our first full-length poetry manuscript.

Any collection of writings will include pieces a reader loves and some they merely tolerate. This book is no exception. But what I love about Darrell's work is its shifting voice. Sometimes he's serious. Sometimes he's quirky.

Many of these poems hit me in the soul, but they represent a significant portion of my life. Some of these poems chronicle his journey once our marriage ended. You'll find your favorites, and you'll have your own reasons to love them.

Angel R. Ackerman
Publisher
November 2021

Contents

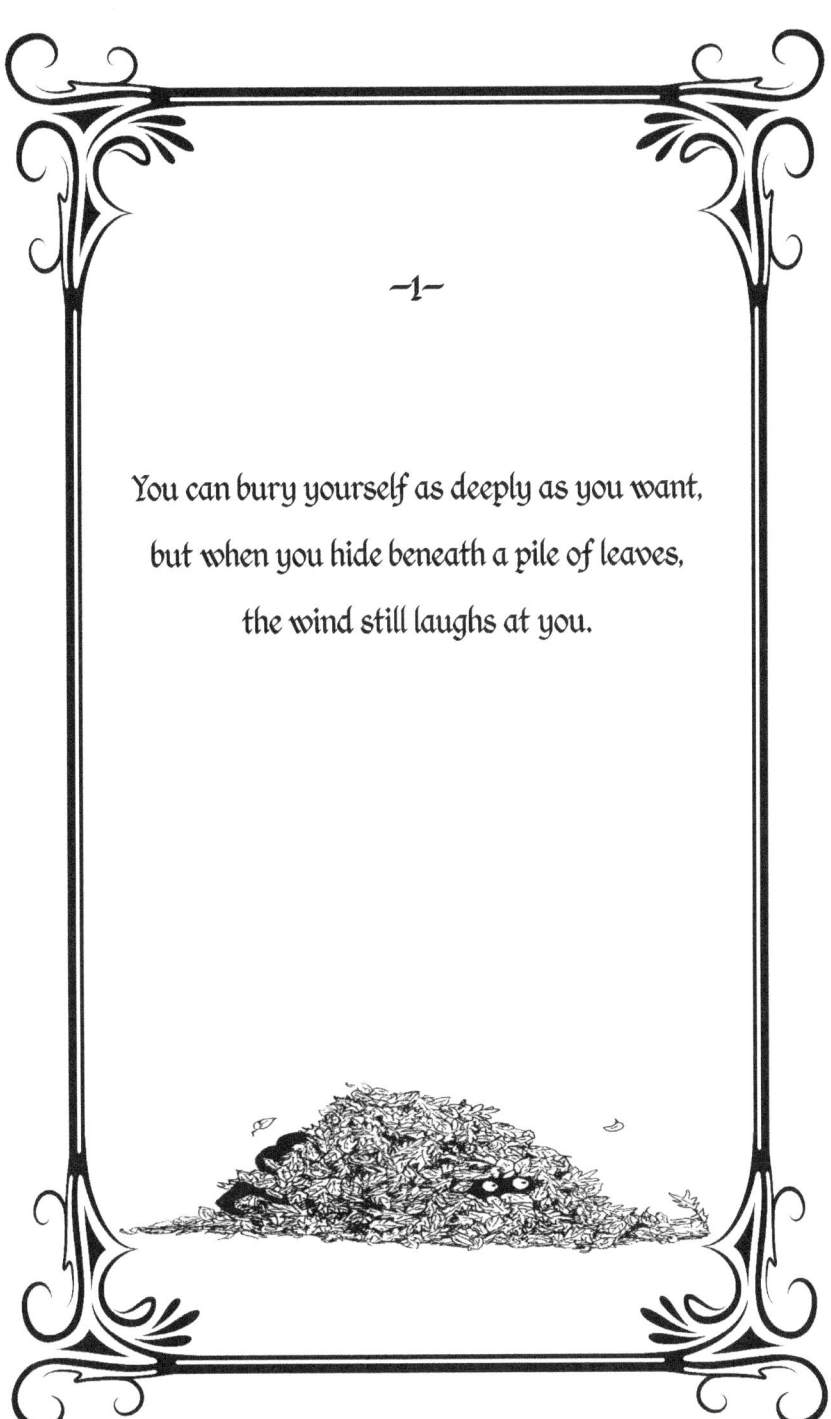

~1~

You can bury yourself as deeply as you want,

but when you hide beneath a pile of leaves,

the wind still laughs at you.

Twists

"You are not like the others."

These words please me
but they are information already incorporated

Not like the others
Not because of the obvious
The physical
Physical twisting of twisted limb
A dead tree branch perhaps still worthy of climbing

Not like the others.
But only because of twists

Twisted, not physically
Twists lingering inside

Not like the others
Because I do things
Wrong things
Twisted things done all the wrong ways

I turn left when straight is better
When straight is more efficient
When straight does not need me
When I know them, know like lovers,
the twists to the left

Zzzzzzzt
Wrong

I take too long
Too long at tasks
Add unnecessary steps
Steps that twist, growing into tasks of their own
Tasks twisting from tasks with steps
twisting every which way
leading to places that I love,
places that bring me peace,
places that the others do not want to go
because they are not like me.

Zzzzzzt
Wrong

I see them
I see always but never up close
close enough to touch
to feel them
I feel but I feel distance.

Curious presence staring from the stars
without emotion without understanding
watching the world twisting through the dark
feeling that I have no part in any of it

Curious presence twisting out in a void
where the others are not
feeling that I have no part in any of it
but that I love it anyway as fish love the sky

The others, the ones I am not like,
they want me to know them
to feel them, to communicate
to converse as they do, but that is something
I never understand

Zzzzzzt
Wrong

Wrong

    Wrong

        Wrong

which is actually right but no one sees it

I am not like the others
That is something they never understand,
something they twist and make their own
carving twisted images of me which are right
but are not actually right

Enter now
suggestions
snarky syllables
endeavors to instruct
to teach me right which is actually wrong
but they don't see it because they are the others
and I am not like them

Enter now: hurtful words
because I am wrong
I am beyond help because I do not give into them

I dance through life
never stopping to see my wrong and their right
or my right and their right
or to see that we are, in fact,
all
    doing
       everything
            wrong!

Because I do see it
That is information already incorporated
but it is something they will never understand
and I forgive them, but do not give in to them

And it makes them angry
and it makes them suggest more
and It makes them use hurtful words more

I do not give in to them but I forgive them
That is something they will never understand
because I am not like the others
Because I forgive them
and I love them for who they are

and this pleases me
because every good story

       every good poem

needs a twist at the end

The Perfect Shade of Weird

A wise friend told me, "I think weird finds weird,"
and nearly convinced me
that I have wasted my life searching.
Though, I am a deep thinker
not so easily swayed.

Weird does find weird.
That is true.
But weird is not a concrete wall.
It has no obvious discernible physical properties.
It is more like a wave
a kind of invisible light,
difficult to define or quantify.
Each individual's wave has a unique pattern of crests and valleys
creating an entire spectrum of weird.

"Weird finds weird," but maybe yours
will find a blue weird
when what it wants is a green.
Maybe that's close enough,
but maybe it's not.

We all crave a weird that will make our weird
feel safe and accepted, tell it that it is beautiful,
dance with it for a spell and perhaps fall in love.

"Weird finds weird."
This is true.
but perhaps what we all seek
is the perfect shade
of weird.

Vacuuming in the Dark

"Do you want the light on to do that?"
 they always say.
 Answer: "No. Not really."
"But how can you see the dirt?"
 Cue the switch click
 Harsh fluorescent glare
—Blinding—
 I continue,
 methodically covering every inch
 of floor in long swishing strokes
 thinking,
"I know I don't have 20/20 vision,
 but if other people can see
 every grain of dirt
 in this multi-colored
 patchwork forest
 of carpet fibers
 perhaps I need
 to start eating more carrots."

Small Things

I made eggs this morning.

Opening the carton
I immediately knew
something was wrong.

Six eggs missing.
Since I live by myself
I had obviously eaten them.

But, while two glistening
white ovals had been removed from
the spaces at each end.

Both remaining unpaired eggs
stared at me from slots
at the back of the carton.

Who touched my eggs?
Left one in Front, Right one in Back so they are in opposite corners.
That is how it works.
Who threw everything out of balance like this?

Nothing made sense about the scenario.
Was someone trying to push me down the slippery slope
into chaos and eventual madness?

I cursed.
I wanted ONE,
but this affront could not go unpunished.
I had to take both rogue eggs now.

Admittedly,
things like this are small,
but they are the key to understanding who I am —
to unlocking the mystery of me
and I realized, at that moment, that I have lived
alone with that knowledge
for far too long.

The Hard Way

What is the proper means
of moving books
from a random disorganized pile
to their places on a shelf?
Most will say,"by the armload, of course!"
"or better yet, with a cart."

Most people do not know books very well.

Books, by their nature, move one copy at a time
from any single fixed location
regardless of the size and scope
of the shelving and how long the trips will be.

Most people consider this the hard way
because they fail to see
how intentional inefficiency
encourages familiarity,
slows the frantic pace of daily life
and brings a Zen-like sense of peace.

Books should do that.

This is one of the many things
books have taught me.

It is also why
I will likely never
be employed
in a library.

The Bus Poem

One day
I just walked out in front of a bus
It didn't take long
(Only about three or four seconds)
before the driver realized what I was doing.
By then it was too late.
Oh, he tried to hit his breaks,
but I think he was going
a little too fast in the first place.

I heard something —
probably my spine —
make a sharp CRACK!
Other than that I only blacked out.
That was disappointing.

Then my friend walked up and asked, "Wathcha doing?"
"Contemplating just walking out in front of this bus," I said.
She gave me a funny look,
"It's already passed."

Glassy-eyed and smiling
I nodded
and my friend
walked on.

Comfortable Creatures

☐ Monday
☐ Tuesday
☐ Wednesday
☐ Thursday
☐ Friday
Yep, all still there.

"But what about Saturday and Sunday?' you ask.
They're less pressing right now.
Perhaps closer to the weekend
I'll revise the list and add them in.

My lists are organic.
They breathe and grow.
I feed them constantly
Like a menagerie of
Chaotic beasts
In habitats of
Random notebooks
Or odd scattered slips.

Sometimes the beasties
Get out of hand.
Tasks break free of their cages.
But when that sort of unexpected
Situation crops up
A quick add and strikethrough
Keeps it at bay.
One more thing off the list.
Even if it wasn't there to start with!
Stressful thoughts
keeping me up at night?
Get up and make a list!
That'll show 'em!

One important note, however:
The denizens of pad and pen
Are but a phylum of my lists.

Wildest and most prolific
By far are the lists in my head.

☐ Wednesday
☐ Thursday
☐ Friday
☐ Saturday
☐ Sunday
I know them, obviously. I don't need to list them.
But I do:
☐ First, I'll have coffee,
☐ Then shower,
☐ Wash up those lingering dishes
☐ No breakfast first, then dishes!
Why make a list of my morning routine
When I do it every day?

Because.

This comfortable practice
Is soothing and versatile
Translating to most anything:
☐ I will wash the bathroom floor
☐ Let that dry
☐ Move to the kitchen floor
☐ Let that dry
☐ Then the dining room
☐ Wait, I don't have a dining room…
Strike another thing off the list!

Sometimes I wonder if I would do anything
Without first putting it on a list.

Perhaps I have discovered the key to immortality.
☐ Lay down and die
☐ Nope, gotta get to the grocery store first.
But the stores are all closed now…
Guess it'll have to wait till tomorrow.
Repeat

Excellent strategy
But the grocery excuse is only good
For a one-time use.
I'll need to come up with more
Tomorrow, perhaps,
I will make a whole list of them.

Feeding Peanuts to the Corvids

Pervasive petrichor on damp heavy air.
The beasts have emerged from shelter
among the cemetery's chestnuts
and sugar maples.

I toss peanuts between the stones
and watch the crows dive and fight
over the tasty treasures.
Chipmunks want a piece of the action,
but opt to sit on the sidelines
and wait for the leftovers,
considering the competition too fierce.

I think if I chose a spirit animal
it would be a crow or a raven.

Sleek, graceful, mysterious
and, of course... black.

But I don't really care for heights
and, anyway, I don't think
you actually get to choose.
Not consciously, at least.

More like the spirit animal chooses you.

On the walk home
I see movement
by the stones
of a squat retaining wall
bordering the path.

A pudgy groundhog
takes note of me
and disappears,
I cannot tell where.
Not a single gap
in the stones
seems big enough
to have swallowed his girth,
yet he is gone.

And I think of the groundhog:
quiet, shy and solitary,
often ignored or unseen.
He just wants to be left alone,
but so often he is shot at
or run over,
flattened by people
on the highway of life.

And suddenly, I know
I've met that spirit animal
I so desperately sought
amidst the tree branches.

Blink

At all the events
and community gatherings
I see them:
The social butterflies
flitting from person to person
landing on hands or shoulders,
sometimes even cheeks or noses.
That is not me.
I am more of a social firefly.
If you work hard enough
and somehow manage to catch me
perhaps I will delight you
by shining briefly
before I raise my wings
and go dark again,
disappearing into the night.
My radiance lingers
only for those willing
to take up the chase.

~2~

Love is feeling unworthy

of the kindness you give to others.

Sock Drawer

I never believed that anyone could want me.
Never imagined why anyone would.
So when she said she thought
that maybe she loved me
I cocked my head curiously at her,
told her that
I didn't know what that meant
or what I was supposed to do,
but that I was willing to try.

I didn't really believe her
even when she kissed me,
blindsided, on my grandmother's couch,
dry mouths like awkward worms
wriggling against one another in parched dirt.

The attempts continued,
but even when the kisses improved,
still, I didn't believe her.
Then came the carte blanche.
The day she told me,
"I think I'd let you do anything to me at this point."

Again, I cocked my head curiously at her
and I replied,
"Do you mean to say
that I could come to your house
and root around in your sock drawer
and you wouldn't mind?"

And that is where 25 years
of communication difficulties began.

Bothering

I'm sitting here
thinking about you
But I don't want to
bother you with it
Because I feel like
I'm sitting here a lot
thinking about you
and I never want to
bother you with it
Because what good would it do
when you've got better things
Important things
A lot on your plate
People who depend on you

I don't depend on you
But I think about you
And I wonder what you're doing
And I care if you're okay
And I care if you're sad
or angry at the world
or wishing there was something more
you could do to make things better.

But you do make things better
for me, anyway.
Just thinking about you
makes things better
and that's why
I never need to
bother you with it.

I just sit here
thinking about you
smiling to myself
and wondering
if maybe it would help
make things better for you
if you knew.

Words

I would give you my soul
If I could find an appropriate hole to let it out.
I would give you my heart
But that's kinda gross.
I would give you my body
But I'll probably be needing that later.
And I would give you my regards
If I had any worth regarding.
Actually, I would give you everything
If I could afford it,
But I can't or I wouldn't or I shouldn't,
Or you wouldn't want me to
And I really don't have much,
So I'll give you my words
and we'll see what happens.

Masterpiece

When I see someone
as artists do,
beauty
is not entirely physical.
It's instinctual
emotional.
Not just colors and shapes
light and shadow.

Because, as with art,
there is an element of abstraction
that change over time.
The more one looks
the more one understands the physical.
A painting may sometimes be lovely
only when seen up close enough
to examine the brushstrokes.

Reality
is up for interpretation
and emotional value,
like color value,
changes perceptions,
casting forms
in different lights.

I could try to explain,
but you'd never believe me
as you come to my door
full of apologies for being disheveled.
But you hug me
and my heart
paints a masterpiece
of you.

Modern Art

You
       Are modern art to me
Your colors are vibrant
and pleasing to see.
       Your shapes are intriguing
Your presence draws me near
            But your meanings are not
   all quite as they appear.

Your
Innate charisma makes me react.
       You seem to make sense
even though you're abstract.
       I want to take you home
         and nail you on the wall
even though I don't
       understand you at all

If She Were a Cat

If she were a cat
she'd be a fickle old calico,
rough and patch-worked,
but beautiful because of it.
She would be
lovable and affectionate,
but flick her tail
from time to time.

Luckily, I'd know
just where to scratch
to make her purr again.

If she were a cat
she'd have the run of the house.
She could lazily lay in the sun
resting all day if she wanted.

I'd let her eat off my plate
and curl up close to me at night.

She'd never be wanting for attention
because petting her supple fur
would be a priceless joy
that I would never sacrifice
to her kitty-cat pride.

Instigator

On the Zoom
I watch the reaction
as you look down
read a secret response to a message
you had whispered on fairy wings of ether.
My words are audible only on your face.

We are looking at one another.
Not that you can tell.
But at the same time
anyone watching can tell
as we struggle, failing to keep
our silly smirks stifled.

You show off your coaster
with Herman Munster.
It's meant for me.
even though anyone can see it,
I know it is mine alone.
And they know it too.

In response,
I stick out my tongue,
positively certain that no one else
will take offense,
thinking it was extended toward them.

You have always been the instigator,
encouraging me in ways no one else ever has,
coaxing me out of the hole I dug for myself
and introducing me to a world
in need of a little mischief.

We're like two children.
Best friends,
flirting teenagers,
laughing with muffled voices
in the back of the classroom
passing notes.

But we aren't children anymore.
Or are we?
Did we ever really grow up?
Because what's the benefit of that?
The job?
The responsibilities?
The money?
The freedom?

It's all a bullshit
and we know it.
And they know it too.
They can see it on our Zoom faces.

Then I'm called on.
My turn to speak
and I say what I have to say
with a confidence
my past-self did not know.
I have their attention—
probably more than I afforded them—
but I no longer get flustered by that.

Then, I look again at you
and your smile assures me
that I'm not a child anymore,
and somewhere
in the deep
grey-green ether
of your eyes

you say,
"Look how far you've come."

and suddenly,
I want to cry.

Closet Creeper

Closet Creeper
Come out and play.
You linger in shadows
But I know you anyway.
You wait to emerge
When everyone sleeps
In the loneliest hours
When no one will see

Closet Creeper
Don't be afraid
I'll shut off the lights
So you can still hide
Closet Creeper
I'm just like you
So why not come out
and sit by my side.

The Love I Feed

The love I feed is a gentle creature.
It does not make demands
or forceful requests.
It seeks only to comfort
console and add quality
to the lives of the objects
of its affection.

The love I feed is a gentle
quiet creature.
It does not speak or make itself seen.
It doesn't make my heart flutter
or keep me up at night
or cause me to skip meals.
That kind of love is fleeting
at best, anyway.

You see,
the love I feed is a gentle,
quiet, steadfast creature.
Complacent and complicit
with the needs of the other.
I have learned
to be careful when allowing
anyone to approach it.
Once it chooses someone,
it's loyalty will not waver
and it affords them
dangerous freedoms.

So, If the love I feed makes eyes at you,
begging for table scraps,
if you are allowed close enough
to feel its warmth and stroke it's fur,
go ahead,
toss it whatever
you might be willing to share.
But only if you're aware
of the responsibility
that entails.

Reciprocating Kindnesses

What if everyone reciprocated kindness
Instead of fighting over parking spaces
Or who gets the last roll of toilet paper
Left on the shelf?
Maybe it's instinct
Like in nature
Each creature in constant conflict
To survive at the expense of the other

Except with humans
it's not survival
It's being further ahead in the queue
We are always placing ourselves in queues
On highways, in stores, on endless phone calls
Forever waiting in lines
Waiting for something
Anything to bring meaning
To our emptiness

But what if everyone reciprocated kindness
Like two friends
Exchanging gifts for no reason
On a crisp fall day
Knowing that who they are
Is invaluable to one another?
What greater meaning
Could there be?

–3–

Screaming at the world will get you nowhere,

but it might make you feel a little bit better.

We Are...

We are liars
as we
tell ourselves
how crucial we are;
> We are mothers.
> We are innocents.
> We are victims.

as we
praise our deeds;
> We are heroes.
> We are saints.
> We are lovers.

or as we
punish our misdeeds;
> We are monsters.
> We are killers.
> We are poets.

While secretly,
we know all along
that at any moment,
fate may strike us down
and let time,
like rain,
wash away
all our dirty footprints.

On Men and Beasts

Posed to me once
was the question
"What separates man from the beasts?"
Given no leave to ponder
I listened
to a lecture on man's intellect
and pension for reason
of man's moral codes and
concerns of spirituality.
And most importantly, he added,
man's lack of natural instincts.

Do we not screw?
Or is that a logical-minded attempt
to keep our precious DNA alive?
Yeah, that's the whole reason.
Everyone wants kids, right?

Do we not fight for dominance?
Or is that only because our moral codes
and concerns of spirituality are correct
whereas those of our enemies are always wrong?

I have a much more succinct answer
should the question ever be posed again
"What separates man from beasts?" you ask?
My answer:
Nothing but man's
positively
ridiculous
over-inflated
ego.

The Wisdom of Screaming

Frustration builds behind steering wheels
with the pressure of airbags straining to expand.

It boils and sizzles on sun-scorched dashboards,
all because some jizz-swilling douche-monkey can't figure out
how to get in a fucking lane!

But as I consider
the impassioned
nonsensical curses
that swirl through my head
I must question the wisdom of screaming.

In today's world strangers' cars follow us everywhere we go.
while our individuality
(Sold by modern culture well below the standard MSRP)
ejects all of them from our personal space
and morphs their faces into anonymous
reflections on windshields.

Well...
except for that arrogant cunt who everyone clearly sees
steering with his elbows while using both hands
to jam a gigantic goddamn cheeseburger down his throat
while merging onto the highway!

Yet, even still, as I observe
The reckless vanity,
blaring horns
and dirty glances in rear view mirrors
I can't grasp the wisdom of screaming.

Everyone likes to feel wronged.
Screamers scream
because they think, perhaps, the small-titted sorority bitch
in front of them
has somehow wronged them
by playing with her cellphone in stopped traffic.

While non-screamers think the impatient assfucker
who honked at them
has wronged them by screaming and waving his hands.
And in their own minds, everyone is right.

But as I glide along this roaring stream
of self-importance,
stocked with iron fish,
I consider the possibility that the wisdom of screaming
does not exist.

Our ears take in screams
as our lungs inhale exhaust fumes:
giving no thought to their harmful implications.

So instead of screaming, I laugh.
I laugh at douche-monkey, cheeseburger face,
sorority bitch, assfucker — all of us
with our ridiculous impersonal, hateful attitudes.

As I stop suddenly
I recognize that I'm alone
within my shadowed interior
watching speed-smeared blurs
buzz past me on the left,
unable to slow their momentum.

And I know,
with a sudden flutter of my heart
that the wisdom of screaming
will always dodge my reason
as an orange tiger-cat
deftly crosses the expressway.

Lines

People hate to wait in lines.
They huff and sigh and tap their feet.

Sometimes they complain
to a minimum-wage earning subhuman
who is only trying to push them through like
mismatched pieces on an assembly line.

It stands to reason that if people honestly hated
to wait in lines
they wouldn't go shopping
for things they didn't really need.
but they do so in droves.

Maybe subconsciously people realize
that what they are buying is not worth
waiting in line for.

Or maybe they think,
for one reason or another,
that they deserve to be ahead of all the other people.

Do you think if there was a line to get into Hell
people still complain about waiting in it?
Or does Lucifer let the complainers move straight to the front
without them having to ask?

Restless

I see your restless spirit
Drowned in life
But rising again and again
Against the dark.
The ghost of you
Preservers against
A reality that ignores your cries
Disbelieves in you
Makes you invisible.
But you cannot be dispelled
And you are dead set
To nag and haunt
It's subconscious
To be recognized
To make yourself known
Even if you have to
Make everything
Burn to do it.

How Did Nora Do Today?

Often, I reflect on how
we skim thousands of lives
during our time in this world,
touching without knowing.

A change of account information
Request of an invoice
We exchange pleasantries,
laugh and joke.

Then afterwards
a survey asks me,
"How did Nora do today?"

I can't answer that.
I didn't even know her name
before this email arrived.
There's no way I am qualified
to comment on her state of being:
her state of "doing!"
How can I be sure it was even "Nora"
I spoke to?

I fill out the survey anyway.
Give her rave reviews.
It probably benefits her some way
in the corporate scheme
of rewards and punishments
that regards employees
as another pack of
Pavlov's dogs.

Later, at the end of the day
I wonder...
How DID Nora do today?

Can she really make ends meet
on a customer service paycheck?

Is her daughter failing Algebra?

Does her dog need surgery?

Is she struggling to keep her marriage alive,
or worse: hiding bruises?

Does she laugh, joke and help
people like me everyday
as if nothing is wrong
while secretly relying on pills
just to get her through the day?

The next day, I call the number again
seeking answers.

A different voice materializes
on the other end of the line.
It seems like
telephones never
connect you with
the same stranger twice.

"How are you doing today?" I ask,
"I need to know, for when I fill out the survey, later."

Capitals

Why didn't I capitalize my name?
Someone proposed self-esteem issues.
But, oh no.

I see people capitalize their names all the time
as if they're better than other nouns.
Maybe they can use more verbs,
adverbs and adjectives
than the other guy.
There's always some explanation...
Some excuse to make them feel bigger,
better, more right.

They capitalize themselves as they capitalize "God."
while never thinking to put one of those
nice leggy letters on "humanity."

As if perhaps "humanity"
should not rank above the individual.

The difference is that
between "God" and "gods."

People capitalize what they believe in
What is more real to them.
Only those close
are ever real to their minds.
The rest of the world's population
is simply the crowd
in the street scene
of a movie:
low paid props
to fill in the gaps in the scenery
behind the important action that affects their lives

People capitalize themselves
without even thinking about it.
It comes naturally, feels right
and it's nothing worth challenging for any one
of the faceless masses of others, right?

Until, perhaps, you come to understand
each of those others
as a god or goddess,
the star of an exclusive, private movie
with a

large,

bold

CAPITALIZED

Title.

Why I'm Walking in the Middle of the Road

Go ahead…
Ask me why I'm walking in the middle of the road
instead of keeping safely off to one side.
And I'll ask you why you stick to the sidewalk
like some discarded wad of chewing gum
Like some pile of mummified dog crap that's
been baking in the sun for three days.
Those who see me may speculate
that I'm a risk taker.
or maybe it's a cry for attention,
they might even think I'm a lunatic.
        But those reasons are highly impractical
and, let's face it, a little fucking cliche.
                The truth is, when I'm walking
                in the middle of the road it's all about awareness.
                Drivers are shocked by my presence.
                They're angry that I'm challenging
the injustice of some people driving around
in posh, air-conditioned SUVs
while others have to hoof it everywhere they go.
                They honk their privileged horns,
                they curse at me and wave their hands,
                but invariably
                they swerve to avoid me
                which is probably for fear of getting dents.
Important note: When they do swerve, they aren't thinking about
where they're going to land.
And that makes all those invisible numbers
        keeping safely off to one side
        nothing
        but unnoticed
        accidental

        targets.

–4–

A List of Things You Should Never Do:

1. Disregard Your Shoes

2. Fail to Pay Tribute to Crows

3. Forget Your Pencil

4. Die

5. Explain Why

6. Dishes

Old Shoes

Don't you hate it…
when you look down at your shoes
and you see how ripped up
scuffed and dirty they are?
And you think back to when you bought them.
"They're practically freakin' new!"

But then
when you think a while longer, you realize
that that day in your memory
was years ago
and now, it's only your crappy
old pair of shoes
that really know
where the time has gone.

Super Blue-Corn Wolf Moon Eclipse

It never fails
some fantastic
cosmic event occurs
in the night sky—
one of those things that only happens
on the fourth Tuesday in July
every seven hundred years or something.

Those occasional times
when I have managed
not to have completely forgotten,
and I have not accidentally
fallen asleep early,
I step out to the porch excitedly
looking upwards ready to be awed

only to observe a dark sky obscured by clouds.

Art is always full of skies
from shining stars to sunsets,
bright piercing shafts of light
streaming from the heavens

But what about the clouds at night
that filter out the moon
make it wispy, milky, shimmering,
no more than a reflection of itself?
What about the clouds
that block out the moon
and stars completely?

Even if I see it all the time,
or at least more often
than the fourth Tuesday in July
every 700 years,

I find the limitless
darkness on darkness
just as beautiful as any other night sky

and I am awed.

Where Things Go

Where do things go when you move?
Who can say?
In an established residence it's obvious.

How did that plastic cup get in with the Tupperware?
It goes next to the coffee mugs.
That is where it has always gone.

You just know... every time
Except for maybe the rebellious catsup
that sometimes moves from the top shelf of the refrigerator door
to the bottom, when the new bottle is too big ...
but mostly, you know.

This changes when you move.
You have to reinvent the entire universe from scratch
putting things in places that you think make sense,
but later can't recall or don't understand.

I know I have raisins.
Why are they not with the crackers, peanuts and other snacks?
Wait, in the pantry with the instant mashed potato flakes?
What was I thinking?
How does THAT make sense?

There is something unsettling about this phenomenon.
In an instant you go from a god in his perfectly ordered universe
to a child who knows nothing and must seek out
and explore as if everything is brand new.

But such is the way of uncertainty
and the choice must be made
to either fear the unknown or
thrill in the discovery.

Corelle

This legacy
bequeathed to me
is not my legacy.
Not my family heirloom dishes
but close enough
for similarities.
For time spent
in that house
with the same amenities.
The same coveted black box
which granted access to all
the pay TV channels
without the prerequisite fees.

Holding a single plate in my hand at the sink,
running tap bubbling soap suds everywhere,
I feel inspired to eat in the living room with my friends
watching cartoons.
Just like old times
when we would
perhaps surf past the porn channel,
no longer just a blur of squiggled
multicolored lines
with uninhibited panting and groaning,
but a grand full frontal view of
all the lurid action that we, as kids,
weren't supposed to see.

That power bequeathed to us
by the technically illegal device
used to define middle-class wealth
in the 1980's,
this privilege
now rendered inert by the internet,
would then, necessarily have compelled us
to turn the volume up up up
just to hear our parents shouts of
"Turn it off!" from the next room
over our chorus of raucous giggles.

Crow's Comedy

On his stage of a tree sat a funny little crow
practicing his comedy routine
I seated myself at a table for one
on a four-foot-high wall made of hard, lumpy stones

The stage lights of morning had barely broken the horizon
as I watched the clown-like up and down bob of his head
In a haphazard pantomime he leapt offstage and then back on
over and over, walking against an invisible wind.

Like a slapstick drunkard he hopped
from branch to branch rising just to fall again
in his unoriginal, yet clever shtick.

Musing screams garbled from his throat
while my breath curled into the air like pungent cigarette smoke
Squawking an unintelligible magic word, he disappeared
Behind a branch only to emerge from the other side.

Then,
>   After his final punch line —
>   one long throaty caw —
>   He made his exit

>   Saying, "Thank you, Thank you!" to my silent applause.

Birds' Funeral

  Flurry
Colors rise
As darkness descends
In sheets of wing-feathers.

They settle on the ground
Near the hollow
Where the dead protrude thick,
Mocking, granite tongues toward heaven.

Near a fresh mound of earth
The tiny, black-clad mourners laugh and ogle.

  "He is dead," they seem to say.
  "Glory to Him on high,
God of birds and God of men,
God of all Gods."

  "At last, he is dead."

The Stone Bench

I went on a walk today
and I found myself sitting
on our stone bench
where we meet
to talk about things.

On my walks
I tend to take the trail
to the spot
where it touches the cemetery.
Often, I cut through
the winding maze of monuments
on the way back home.

Today my route took me
on that course.
Now I'm sitting on the chill
of that stone seat thinking.

If I should die early
don't ever bother
visiting my grave.
Wherever they may
end up planting me
doesn't matter.

Instead, come here.
Sit on this smooth stone
and remember me.

And I promise to be here
sitting beside you.

Exorcism

After the supernatural thriller
on Netflix I should really
have known better
than to try and clean my fridge.

I think all the ghosts in my house
reside in the refrigerator.

I can see the remnants
of the poltergeists' untold
havoc and destruction
amid the jars and bottles
of condiments in the door,

hear the raspy whispers
echoing through
ancient leftover containers,

and sense those silent spirits
that haunt the no-man's land
between the jellies and the salsa.

But unlike any ghost-hunter or
paranormal investigator on TV
I have no EMF detectors,
no night-vision video cameras,
no voice recorders to gather EVP.
I have no blessed crosses,
or spells or magic crystals.

I go in armed only
with a dishrag and soapy water.
to exorcise my demons
and purge the evil from my home.

Procession

Twisty back roads
55 miles per hour.
Then, suddenly,
red and blue lights at the intersection.
I don't have time for this.
Shit.
Funeral.
I sit, foot irritated
on the brake.
They go by
slowly
each with a tiny flag.
Damned Funeral

Next Car:
Somber Gentlemen
in black formal wear.

Next Car:
Blue-Haired Old Women
gossiping wildly about the
deceased's personal life.

Next Car:
A Man in a Tacky Polo Shirt
his wife, smiling next to him as if
he just cracked a joke.

I stop,
fiddle with the radio to kill time
I look up again.

Next Car:
A Middle-Aged, Bald Man
with his index finger shoved
way up his left nostril.
The guy in the Hearse
Should be glad
He doesn't have to witness this.
I'll bet he's smiling right now
and breathing a sigh of relief.
Because his wait is over
while I'm
still
sitting
here.

Lucky Stiff

Haunted

My still, granite eyes lie indecorously
As a distant, glazed monument to solitude.
— Thought can make a tomb of a carnival –

The world outside the gates of concentration
Chatters and bustles with
Minor moments from everyday lives
As I sit strewn in my shadowy silence.

Weaving ancient arts, I commiserate
With the spirits that haunt the derelict shack
In which my imagination dwells.

I console, intimidate, or mock as necessary,
Taunting those unruly poltergeists
Who dance and sway in my subconscious
Like the rhythms of leaves whispering in the wind.

Eventually, they will reveal their grave-guarded secrets
And lead me groping through the darkness
Until I finally touch the perfect magic word to complete
The latest epitaph to my stagnant creativity.

Marks

Anxious,
pensive
and inspired
Searching pockets
for implements
to make thought into a permanent mark.
        Finding none
I try over and over again
to sink elusive syllables
deeper into my mind's reservoir

Finding failure drawing close
I think,
hope
that perhaps
if I scuff my sneakers
in quick, hard strokes
        with enough savage resolve
maybe
phrase by
        splintering
                fading
phrase
I can scrape a few lines
        of a poem
                onto the sidewalk.

Excuses, Excuses

Okay, look, no more excuses!
Got it?
Starting right now!

But, what are excuses all about, really?
Did you ever do that thing
where you use excuses
to cover for your reasons
because you think your reasons
are going to sound like excuses?

It happens.
If we need to bow out of something
and we are embarrassed to talk
about our social anxiety
or we don't want to sound like we're complaining
about having to pick the kids up from band practice
or about desperately needing to do laundry,
we think that
"I have to work," or "I have an appointment"
is easier to swallow than whatever
legitimate factors impact our decision-making.

It's like we assume that
they'll assume
that we just don't want to go
rather than recognize
the everyday complexities
that make up our lives.

Chances are they wouldn't,
or they might.
We don't know because this is our culture.
This is our social disconnect!

Instead of being honest with one another
we replace the reality
of our situations with lies
because we fear judgment.

So we casually fashion fictions
so that others will never really know
who we are and what motivates us.

We exist in a space
where our reasons
make us feel inadequate
and our excuses
are a shield
that makes us feel safe
and protected
from what other people
MIGHT
think.

Do we not see something wrong with this equation?
Of course we do!
But we keep doing it
and I'll tell you why...
I'll be up writing all night if you let me,
but you know what? I won't.

Actually,
I can't even think about this anymore right now.
I'm getting a headache.

Darrell Parry founded the online publication *Stick Figure Poetry Quarterly* and hosts numerous open mics, festivals and other writing-related events. He scatters his work around in a few online magazines and various video recordings for special events, but focuses mainly on live performances. His non-poetic alter ego works in higher education, not a professor, but as one of those reviled peddlers of unaffordable course materials. Believe it or not, in his adventures as a bookseller, he even sometimes sells poetry.

Where to find him . . .

Online Publications:
River and South Review, Winter 2020
Stick Figure Poetry Quarterly, Spring 2020
Feral: A Journal of Poetry and Art. Issue eleven, December 2021

Various recorded performances and panel discussions
Eastonbookfestival.org

▶ Icehouse Tonight: youtube.com/watch?v=ELt0zzLHgrY

Read his journal *Stick Figure Poetry Quarterly*
stickfigurepoetry.com

Find events he hosts and participates in by following

⌾ Stick_Figure_Poetry
ⓕ StickFigurePoetryQuarterly
ⓕ groups/1430565513649816

⊕ lehighvalleypoetry.org

Addendum

If I Knew I was Gonna Live This Long I'd 've Taken Better Care of Myself

We heard him say
these phrases so often
in times of trouble.

"That's life in the fast lane."

"Take it easy, It ain't the end o' the world.
Ya know what I mean?"

"Well, You're the in pretty good shape
for the shape you're in."

These idioms were not new or unique,
but the crass sincerity with
which they were muttered
took you off guard.

He had a way of mocking pain
and attacking the cause
with simple wisdom
that would make you laugh
in spite of yourself.

It wasn't what he said, but the way he said it.
He wasn't wrong, but his matter-of-fact
Brusqueness would usually get him scolded
for being the one to give voice to the logic.

When he told an off-color joke
or made an inappropriate comment
in the face of a supposed tragedy
he'd add, "You gotta laugh or you'll cry."
And whether you agreed with his methods or not,
in the end, you usually felt a little bit better.

I remember when he came
to fix his daughter's old beat-up Ford Escort
for the millionth time,
asking, "You got a screwdriver?"
"No? How about a paperclip or somethin'?"

When she questioned why he never brought tools
he told her, "Any idiot can fix it with tools."

This made sense.
Difficult situations didn't phase him
and he didn't need tools to deal with them.

Not screwdrivers
Not empathy.
Not anything but his irreverent philosophy.

If he knew we were grieving for him right now
he'd probably cock one eyebrow, his mouth agape
in a ridiculous mockery of shock.
He would belt out a laugh and say something like,
"Ya didn't think I was planning on living forever, did ya?"

And he wouldn't be wrong,
but we would still scold him
for being the one to give voice to it.

And whether you agreed with his methods or not,
you might just laugh along with him
in spite of your heavy heart
and maybe even feel a little bit better for it.

Acknowledgments

Many thanks to my production team at Parisian Phoenix:

Angel Ackerman, who nudged me into doing this crazy book thing in the first place and lent her editorial expertise to the project. She has always pushed me in good directions, even if I sometimes made her push a little too hard. Gayle F. Hendricks, font queen and graphic editor in charge pasting all the pieces together to resemble a real book. Mayann Riker, whose phenomenal watercolor adorns the cover.

Gratitude, also to the various poetry communities that have welcomed me over the past 5 years or so, locally and nationwide via zoom. The work they do supporting each other, supporting indie press and providing spaces for people who have words festering inside in need of release is of immeasurable importance. Special shout-out to Lynn Alexander for opening me up to those communities by pointing out that, yes, there are, in fact, things that happen on the other side of my front door if I venture out and look around.

I would be quite remiss if I didn't give a big thanks to my kiddo, Eva Parry, for helping to launch Stick Figure Poetry's website, hosting and attending Open Mics and being a test ear to try out new material. Her support of my writing started very early (even before the day she found my old notebook and said with wonder, "I didn't know Daddy wrote poetry!") and it has continued to this day.